THE NATIVITY OF OUR LORD

from the series
The Twelve Great Feasts for Children

by Sister Elayne
with illustrations by Bonnie Gillis

CONCILIAR PRESS
Ben Lomond, California

The Nativity of Our Lord
from ***The Twelve Great Feasts for Children*** series

Poems © copyright 2002 by Sister Elayne
Illustrations © copyright 2002 by Bonnie Gillis

Published by   Conciliar Press
                P.O. Box 76
                Ben Lomond, California 95005

Printed in Romania

ISBN 1-888212-36-5

The Feast of the
Nativity of Our Lord
is celebrated on December 25.

"Thy Nativity, O Christ our God, hath shone
to the world the light of wisdom!
For by it, those who worshipped the stars
were taught by a star to adore Thee,
the Sun of Righteousness, and to know Thee,
the Orient from on high.
O Lord, Glory to Thee."
— *Troparion of the Feast*
of the Nativity of Our Lord

Be glad! Be glad! For on this day
The Virgin in a manger lays
Her newborn Son, an Infant small,
And worships Him as God of all!

Now Mary looks with tender love
On Christ, who came down from above,
And asks her Son, "How can this be,
That I have given birth to Thee!"

And Joseph with a holy fear
To Mary's little Boy draws near
And thinks on this amazing thing—
The Virgin's Son is Heaven's King.

The shepherds hear the angels sing
The praises of our God and King
And run with gladness to the cave
That holds the One who comes to save.

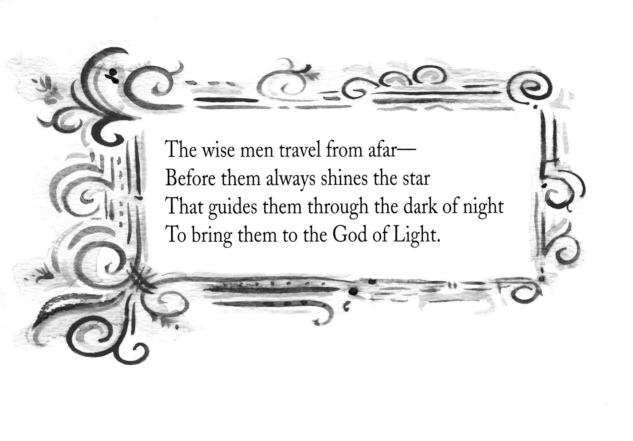

The wise men travel from afar—
Before them always shines the star
That guides them through the dark of night
To bring them to the God of Light.

But Herod's heart with hatred fills.
So in his evil pride he kills
The infants, but his mad design
Cannot destroy the Child Divine.

No! Jesus' life is safe until
He lays it down of His own will
For He has come to earth to die
And raise us up with Him on high!

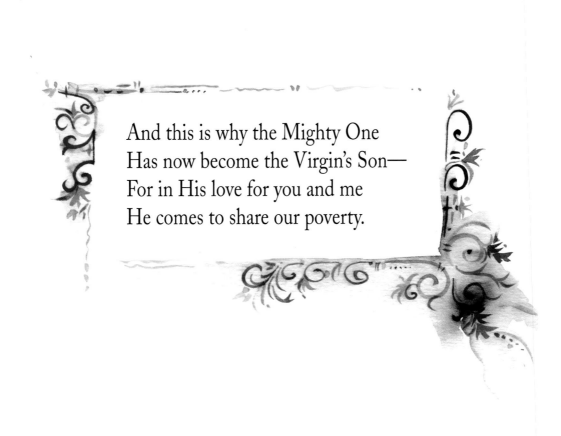

And this is why the Mighty One
Has now become the Virgin's Son—
For in His love for you and me
He comes to share our poverty.

But He wants more than just to live
With us. He also comes to give
The Life of God to Adam's race
And so He makes us gods by grace.

Be glad! Be glad then, everyone!
For our salvation has begun.
Yes! God has come with us to dwell—
A Babe, our King—Emmanuel!

ABOUT THE AUTHOR AND ILLUSTRATOR:

Sister Elayne is a member of the community of St. Barbara Orthodox Monastery in Santa Barbara, California.
Bonnie Gillis is an iconographer and illustrator. She currently lives in San Dimas, California, where she and her husband,
Deacon Michael, attend St. Peter Antiochian Orthodox Church.

ABOUT THE SERIES:

In the Orthodox Church Year, the Feast of Feasts, in a class by itself, is the Resurrection. After the Resurrection in importance come
the Twelve Great Feasts. These feasts are the Church's celebration of, and participation in, key events leading to our salvation. The
Great Feasts are commonly separated into Feasts of the Lord and Feasts of the Theotokos (the Mother of God).

Feasts of the Lord

Exaltation of the Cross
Nativity of Our Lord (Christmas)
Theophany of Our Lord (Epiphany)
Entry of Our Lord into Jerusalem (Palm Sunday)
Ascension of Our Lord
Pentecost
Transfiguration of Our Lord

Feasts of the Theotokos

Nativity of the Theotokos
Entry of the Theotokos into the Temple
Meeting of Our Lord (Presentation of Christ in the Temple)
Annunciation
Dormition of the Theotokos

In this series, we use simple verse and colorful illustrations to acquaint children with the themes and imagery of each of these feasts.
We hope that this provides the children a groundwork for experiencing the joy and wonder of these truly Great Feasts.